THE BUBONIC
PLAGUE

Essential Events

The Bubonic

Plague

BY KEVIN CUNNINGHAM

Content Consultant
Lester K. Little,
professor emeritus of history, Smith College
director emeritus, American Academy in Rome

ABDO
Publishing Company

CREDITS

Published by ABDO Publishing Company, 8000 West 78th Street,
Edina, Minnesota 55439. Copyright © 2011 by Abdo Consulting
Group, Inc. International copyrights reserved in all countries. No
part of this book may be reproduced in any form without written
permission from the publisher. The Essential Library™ is a
trademark and logo of ABDO Publishing Company.

Printed in the United States of America,
North Mankato, Minnesota
112010
012011

♻ THIS BOOK CONTAINS AT LEAST 10% RECYCLED MATERIALS.

Editor: Mari Kesselring
Copy Editor: Paula Lewis
Interior Design and Production: Kazuko Collins
Cover Design: Christa Schneider

Library of Congress Cataloging-in-Publication Data
Cunningham, Kevin, 1966-
  The bubonic plague / by Kevin Cunningham.
    p. cm. -- (Essential events)
  Includes bibliographical references and index.
  ISBN 978-1-61714-762-3
  1. Plague--History--Juvenile literature. 2. Plague--Europe--
History--Juvenile literature. 3. Plague--Asia--History--Juvenile
literature. 4. Black Death--Juvenile literature. I. Title.
  RC172.C85 2011
  614.5'732--dc22
                                    2010043852

TABLE OF CONTENTS

Plague victims were often buried together in large pits because there was not enough time or space to dig separate graves.

DEATH IN AVIGNON

uy de Chauliac served as one of the physicians to Pope Clement VI, head of the Roman Catholic Church from 1342 to his death in 1352. At the time, political problems had driven the Church from Rome, Italy, to Avignon, a city in the south of France. Religious pilgrims, Church leaders, nobles, and their helpers and followers streamed into the city on a daily basis. A booming population of tailors, merchants, innkeepers, and others made a living serving them.

A disease crept into Avignon at the close of 1347. Or, rather, it scampered, brought in by black rats. No one thought much of it when the first victims died in January 1348. But the bodies soon began to pile up and people were concerned. City authorities did not recognize the illness. Neither did Chauliac, one of France's most respected medical minds.

Nor did anyone understand how it was spread from person to person. The ancient medicine used by medieval physicians and surgeons had no effect on the illness. As Chauliac wrote:

Astrology

Astrology played an important, if wrong-headed, role in medieval medicine. A physician's visit usually started with drawing up the patient's horoscope. The patient's astrological background influenced the physician's opinion on their problems as well as possible treatments. Many physicians never examined the patient's body.

[I]t was futile and shameful for the physicians, in that they did not dare visit their patients for fear of infection, and when they did visit them, they cured none and gained nothing; for all the patients died, except a few toward the end who escaped with burned out buboes.[1]

What Is It?

Chauliac noted two forms of the disease. The first, and far deadlier of the two, affected the lungs. Patients became feverish and coughed up blood. The second form caused fever too. But the telltale symptom was the painful egg-shaped swellings, or buboes, under the arms, in the groin, and on one side of the neck by the ear.

Chauliac recognized that the first form of the disease was contagious. Because it spread from person to person, he advised Pope Clement to avoid contact with others. As

"None of the earlier epidemics were as severe, since they occupied a single region, while this involved the entire world; the others were curable in some manner, this by none."[2]

—*Guy de Chauliac*

Chauliac also held the common belief that "bad air" caused disease, he told the pope to sit between two roaring fireplaces. He explained that the smoke would cleanse the room of sickness.

All across Avignon, townspeople hacked up blood, stumbled through feverish hazes, and died on their feet or after days of suffering. Bonfires lit to purify the air sputtered and crackled. Pigs and dogs dug up newly buried corpses. So many people died that the cemeteries ran out of space. With Pope Clement's permission, the grave diggers threw the bodies in the local river.

Guy de Chauliac

Guy was born around the year 1300 in the tiny village of Chauliac. Since France had yet to adopt the custom of last names, he became known as Guy *de Chauliac*, meaning "of Chauliac." Upon leaving home, Chauliac attended the best medical schools in France. He became what was called a master of medicine. No one yet used the term *doctor*.

Chauliac wanted to become a surgeon. Medieval society considered surgery a trade like that of a carpenter or a shipbuilder. Chauliac's medical instructors probably shook their heads at an educated man becoming a tradesman. But Chauliac saw surgery as a way to better understand medicine. His interest in anatomy, the study of the structures of the body, led him to a famed surgical school in Bologna, Italy.

During his career, Chauliac served at least three popes and taught at one of France's major medical schools. He found lasting fame, however, after his death. His seven-volume masterpiece, *Great Surgery*, became the main textbook for Western European surgeons for the following 300 years.

Pope Clement VI

Chauliac claimed the outbreak lasted seven months. During the winter, the form that attacked the lungs dominated. As the weather warmed, a second strain, with the buboes, became more common. By the end of the outbreak, the pope had fled the city. Virtually everyone with the money or means to do so did the same. But Chauliac stayed. "And I, in order to avoid a bad reputation, did not dare depart," he wrote.[3] He paid for his decision. In the summer, he fell ill with fever and buboes. His illness lasted six weeks, but he survived.

Chauliac and other educated writers referred to the time as "the Great Mortality" or "the Great Dying." The average European called the disease "the pest." Centuries later, historians gave it the name the Black Death. Today, people generally refer to the disease as the bubonic plague.

Unfortunately, Avignon was just one of the major cities to suffer from a plague epidemic. For centuries the bubonic plague would torment citizens throughout Asia, Europe, the Middle East, and eventually the United States. Only a few continents

Supernatural Causes

Observers of the time believed supernatural events caused or at least foretold disasters. Louis Sanctus, a musician in Avignon, heard plague originated in India after strange events struck the region. One day, according to the story, it rained snakes, scorpions, and other venomous animals. On the next day, storms dropped huge hailstones. The third day brought fire and smoke that destroyed all living things. Thereafter, the region became infected with a disease. According to the story, winds carried disease to ships that then moored in Italy and France.

would be spared from the deadly disease that so often left its victims dead. Outbreaks of plague would inspire art, literature, and music. It would shake the faith of the people, leading them to question their church and government leaders, place blame on innocent citizens, and even doubt their god. Plague would alter the course of human history, and it would never be the same. ⌐

Guy de Chauliac

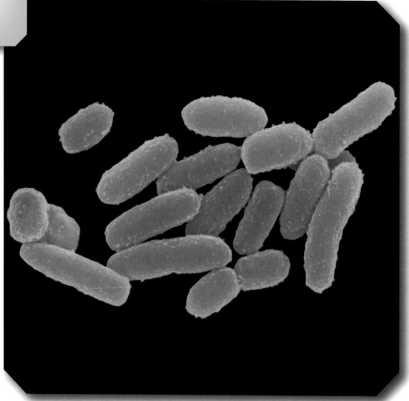
Yersinia pestis

THE ADVERSARIES

Experts believe the plague-causing bacterium, *Yersinia pestis,* first infected rodents in China and seems to have evolved from a related bacterium within the last 20,000 years. An alternative theory proposed the disease began in East

Africa. However, in 2010, scientist Mark Achtman and his team at University College Cork in Ireland used genetics research to conclusively prove that *Y. pestis* originated in China.

PLAGUE, RODENTS, AND FLEAS

Y. pestis, like any bacterium, needs a host so it can reproduce. A host is a living thing that the bacterium lives in and infects. For *Y. pestis*, rodents became the host. Bubonic plague is still mainly a rodent disease. It is found in giant gerbils in central Asia, guinea pigs in Ecuador, prairie dogs in the United States, bandicoot rats in India, and other species on every settled continent except Australia.

For the most part, *Y. pestis* moves back and forth between the rodents it infects and the fleas that carry the bacteria. Often the infected rodents do not die. But on occasion, plague may wipe out huge numbers of a rodent species. For example, the US government estimated that 98 percent of North American prairie dogs died of a combination of plague and human extermination efforts in the twentieth century. If the plague-carrying fleas move to a species that lives near cities or near people, the disease may encroach into human society.

At least 80 kinds of fleas carry *Y. pestis*. When it comes to plague, the bacterium's most important ally is the Oriental rat flea (*Xenopsyla cheopis*). The Oriental rat flea is what scientists call a vector—an animal that carries a disease-causing agent and passes it on to humans.

Fleas feed on the blood of other animals. Each species of flea has its favorite food source. *Pulex irritans*, the human flea, prefers people. The Oriental rat flea, as the name implies, feeds on rodents. An Oriental rat flea sucks up *Y. pestis* from an infected rodent as it feeds. If the flea leaps to another rodent, it can pass along the bacterium when it

A Flea's Life

Xenopsyla cheopis, like all fleas, is a great survivor. Armor makes it tough; its ability to jump 100 times its own height makes it mobile; and the spiny structures on its body allow it to hang onto the fur or hair of a mammal host.

A rat flea tends to remain on one host throughout its three-month life cycle. If the host dies, however, the flea must find another host. The rat flea, if forced, can make its new home on many mammals, including human beings. If unable to find a host, *X. cheopis* can hibernate underground for up to a year as it waits for another suitable host.

An infected flea may live its life without showing any effects of the *Y. pestis* bacteria inside it. At times, however, the bacteria reproduce so wildly they block the insect's digestive system. Soon, the flea can no longer eat. As starvation sets in, it bites its host over and over in a desperate attempt to feed. Each time it does, it regurgitates bacteria into the host. For a long time, scientists believed that only blocked fleas spread plague. More recent research has questioned that idea. Finding an answer would solve one of the many mysteries that still surround plague.

feeds on its new host. This is the main way bubonic plague spreads in both rodents and in humans.

One Disease, Three Forms

Bubonic plague is one of the few diseases that kill five or six out of every ten humans who catch it. Yet it is the mildest of the disease's three forms. Despite its fearsome reputation, bubonic plague is not very contagious. It usually infects humans through a flea bite. On rare occasions, it enters through a cut or other break in the skin.

Once in the body, the *Y. pestis* bacteria use the bloodstream to seek out the lymph nodes. Plague favors the lymph nodes located in the groin, under the arms, on the neck, or behind the ears. As bacteria reproduce in the lymph nodes, the organs swell into buboes like those observed by Chauliac. The infected person may also suffer from fever, chills, extreme exhaustion, and headaches.

A bubo is incredibly painful. Even small movements can bring on agony. As the disease advances, the tissue around the buboes may begin to rot. In other cases, however, the bubo hardens and bursts. Pus pours from the wound. The person may then start to recover.

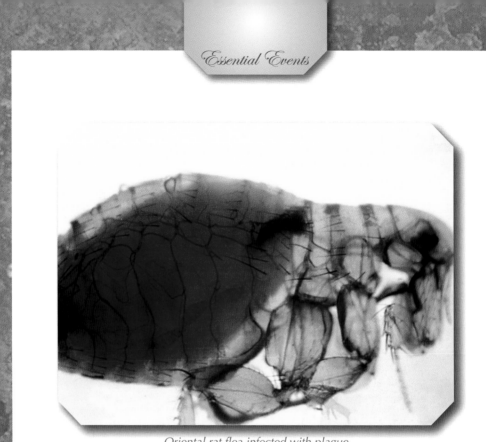

Oriental rat flea infected with plague

The second plague form, pneumonic plague, is less common and more deadly. It spreads in two ways. Sometimes *Y. pestis* introduced by a flea bite settles in the lungs after striking the lymph nodes. More often, pneumonic plague spreads when an infected victim coughs out blood teeming with plague bacteria and another person breathes in an infected particle of fluid.

Pneumonic plague impacts the lungs like super-pneumonia. In some cases, symptoms start just hours after the person inhales the bacteria, though the process can take three or four days. The victim feels pain in the chest. It becomes more difficult to breathe as the lungs fill with fluid. Body temperature shoots up. Sometimes the person feels weak and may become nauseated or start vomiting. Unless treated quickly with modern drugs, a pneumonic plague patient will die of a combination of internal bleeding, shock, and lung or heart failure.

The rarest form of plague, septicemic plague, infects the bloodstream. It develops from bubonic plague or by itself after a flea bite. Septicemic plague causes symptoms similar to the bubonic and pneumonic forms. It also causes severe bleeding internally and from the mouth, nose, and rectum. Gangrene can affect the arms, legs, nose, and ears. Without treatment, septicemic plague always kills its

Plague's Meanings

The ancient Greek word *plaga* meant "a strong blow," such as being hit by a sword or a fist. The Greeks of that era, increasingly exposed to new and frightening afflictions, adapted the word into *plague* to refer to any contagious disease. Not until the 1800s did *plague* come to mean a disease caused by the bacterium *Y. pestis*. Some people today still use *plague* as a synonym for any harmful disease.

victims. It remains dangerous today despite the existence of effective medicines. Without treatment, people usually die within 15 hours of showing symptoms.

Disease Pools

The bacteria and parasites that cause disease evolve and thrive in certain ecosystems, just as animals and plants do. Matching up with a reliable host organism, as *Y. pestis* did with rodents, allows some bacteria to remain around long enough to cause issues for human beings.

As a pathogen—that is, a disease-causing virus, bacterium, parasite, or fungus—adapts to its host, it develops relationships with other organisms. These relationships, in turn, affect various parts of the ecosystem.

Historian William McNeill studied areas where certain pathogens developed such relationships with animals as well as humans. He called these areas "disease pools." Disease pools are unique as each has its own pathogens. For example, the disease pool located in a region of East Africa had its own pathogens. The country of Mongolia in north-central Asia also has a unique set of pathogens.

A disease that is constantly present in an area is considered endemic. Sometimes, an endemic disease circulates only in animals. Scientists call the host animal species the "reservoir" for a disease. Marmots in Asia, for example, became a reservoir for plague in prehistoric times. An endemic disease may or may not cause problems for humans. Even when it does, it is possible only very few people become infected. However, this was not the case with plague.

First Humans Infected

The first occurrences of plague seem to have taken place in China. At first, the disease remained confined to the lands where it evolved. But changes and advancements in human societies eventually gave plague an opportunity to extend its reach. New technologies and a hunger for trade encouraged ancient cultures

Marmots

The bobak marmot and tarabagan marmot are two Asian rodents believed to have an ancient relationship with plague. Humans have hunted both animals for their meat and fur for centuries. People in Manchuria and other parts of Asia have long recognized that marmots carry plague. Experienced hunters avoid slow-moving marmots because sluggishness is a sign of infection. Scientists believe marmots were the source of a pneumonic plague outbreak that devastated Manchuria from 1910 to 1911. Occasional marmot-related cases still occur today.

from China to Egypt to Italy to forge links with one another. The technologies and trade produced a give-and-take of ideas and products—and diseases.

Black rats and other rodents carry plague to humans.

Emperor Justinian, center, in a mosaic at the Church of San Vitale in Italy

JUSTINIAN'S PLAGUE

housands of years ago, a pathogen rarely escaped its disease pool because humans lived in small groups and seldom traveled far from home. But that changed as explorers ventured into distant lands. Buddhist missionaries crossed from

India to China more than 2,200 years ago. Chinese merchants carried their goods across central Asia. From as early as 500 BCE, and thereafter, Greek armies and merchants traveled through Persia, the Middle East, and the Black Sea region.

The contact between these people, who carried pathogens from different disease pools, increased. No one knows how or when plague escaped its disease pool. But it is clear when it arrived in Europe and the Middle East.

PLAGUE ARRIVES IN CONSTANTINOPLE

In 527 CE, the Byzantine Empire was the major power in the Mediterranean. Its new emperor, Justinian, was the most ambitious ruler of his era. His seven-hilled capital, Constantinople, was the hub of a trading and military empire. Justinian's greatest desire was to

Disease Invaders

Deadly pathogens frequently entered the Mediterranean disease pool during the time of the Roman Empire. Roman soldiers returning from Mesopotamia (modern-day Iraq) carried the Antonine Plague in 165 CE. The Antonine Plague was not bubonic plague but smallpox or measles. In addition to killing thousands in Rome, the disease was carried on the empire's road system and shipping routes to other regions. The Cyprian Plague, also probably smallpox, struck in 251 CE and continued off and on for decades.

revive the Western Roman Empire. Therefore, the Byzantines battled the many armies that sought control of Italy. At the same time, Justinian's armies faced the powerful Sassanian Persians. During this time, Constantinople depended on Egypt to provide many goods. However, in addition to grain, cloth, and ivory, Egypt may have sent a far less desirable export—*Rattus rattus*—the black rat.

Also called the Alexandrine rat, the roof rat, and the ship rat, the species originated in India. Black rats usually travel in groups. Sometimes a colony sleeps together in a large heap. The black rat's legendary climbing ability allows it to run

Animal Diseases

Plague is only one of many human diseases that evolved first in animals. Scientists call a disease that crosses from animals to human a zoonosis. Experts consider humans a dead-end host for plague. In other words, plague crosses to human beings but eventually burns itself out and returns to infecting its animal hosts. Other zoonotic diseases include the West Nile virus (from birds) and rabies (from various mammals).

Influenza, however, is a zoonosis that has become a full-fledged human disease. In the past, influenza infected the intestines of ducks. As Asian farmers began to keep ducks as livestock, influenza crossed over to human beings. It now circulates in the human population full-time. Other hosts such as water birds and pigs often pass along new kinds of influenza as well.

Many familiar diseases made a similar leap. Measles may have originated in cattle. Anthrax probably evolved in cows, sheep, or their wild relatives. HIV may have begun as a disease of chimpanzees.

straight up a 90-degree surface. On sailing ships, it climbed on the masts and rigging. On land, it nested in attics, roofs, and tangles of vines on the sides of buildings. The black rat arrived in Europe no later than ancient times, and perhaps even earlier. Because the species had lived in Europe for so long and was a well-established species, it was the perfect host to spread plague when *Y. pestis* reached the Mediterranean disease pool.

It is not clear where plague first broke out. In 541, however, it reached Pelusium, a port on the Mediterranean Sea. According to Procopius, a Byzantine historian of the time, it spread from Pelusium in two directions—toward the rest of Egypt to the west and Palestine to the east.

Some historians suspect that Egyptian grain opened doors for the disease in Constantinople. The government stored grain in four immense warehouses. The mountains of food inside drew masses of black rats and other rodents. Even the flea population benefited. Grain dust was a favorite meal of the Oriental rat flea's young. As the rat population increased, so did the flea population. It is possible that humans handling the grain were bitten by the insects and infected.

In Constantinople, plague spread slowly at first. The winter temperatures killed the Oriental rat flea. But, in the spring of 542, plague began to kill the city's rats. Swarms of fleas went in search of new hosts. Plague reached Constantinople's human population that same year. As Procopius described, many of those infected were not even aware they had a fatal illness:

> They had a sudden fever. . . . And the body [showed] no change from its previous color, nor was it hot as might be expected when attacked by a fever, nor indeed did any [swelling] set in. . . . It was natural, therefore, that not one who contracted the disease expected to die from it.[1]

However, Procopius noted that the disease soon intensified:

> [A] bubonic swelling developed; and this took place not only . . . below the abdomen, but also inside the armpit, and in some cases also beside the ears, and at different points on the thighs.[2]

Procopius also noticed that disease affected different people in different ways. Some fell into a coma or suffered total exhaustion. Many could not recognize friends or loved ones. There were even cases where victims, frightened by imaginary enemies, ran screaming into the street.

By late spring, the poor and the rich alike were dying. Procopius recorded that 5,000 people died per day during the epidemic's peak, though this estimate may not be accurate. Trade slowed and then stopped completely. Taxes went uncollected, businesses stayed closed. Hunger became a problem because the city's food producers, such as bakers, were sick, dead, or too terrified to leave home.

The Helpless City

Byzantine physicians were mystified over how the disease spread since it did not seem to be contagious among people. No one had any idea that the black rats in the streets played a part. Nor could the wisest healers imagine flea bites and bacteria as causes.

Getting rid of the dead presented an enormous challenge. At first, only the most desperate dared

Beyond Constantinople

John of Ephesus, a clergy-man and writer, landed in Alexandria, Egypt, at about the same time the disease appeared. Plague moved east even as he traveled into Palestine and Syria. In the aftermath, John saw towns and farms emptied by the disease. "We used to face the grave during the whole day as we looked at the devastated and moaning villages in these regions," he wrote, "and at corpses lying on the ground with no one to gather them."[3]

to take a job disposing of bodies. Eventually, Justinian commanded his soldiers to join in the effort. When the cemeteries were full, soldiers dug trenches and pits and placed the dead in layers. But soon there was no place left to dig. Bodies were stacked on barges and floated out to sea to await burial. The corpses then went into the water. Currents later washed the corpses up on the shoreline. Soldiers in one part of Constantinople dumped the dead into the towers of a local fortress.

The First Pandemic

Even Emperor Justinian became infected by the bubonic plague, though he survived. However, the plague named after him became a pandemic, spreading all over the world. Over the next year, in 543, the disease spread to Italy, Spain, southern France, and what is modern-day Croatia. Byzantine trade and military links carried the disease east to Persia and Armenia.

Lost Ambitions

Justinian's Plague left Byzantium weakened and poorer. The emperor had lost many of his military and civil leaders. The merchant ships had no one to sail them. Orchards died, desert monasteries sat empty, and farmland went unplowed. Plague had taken the experts Justinian needed to run his empire and the taxpayers he needed to pay for his wars. Enemies, aware of the empire's weakness, attacked Byzantium from both the east and west. By the time Justinian died in 565, his grand plan to restore the Roman Empire of old had ended in failure.

Y. pestis soon established itself in the fleas and rats of Mediterranean Europe, Africa, and the Middle East.

This pandemic, now called the First Pandemic, continued into the eighth century. Historians who studied writings of the time suggest that plague arrived on a ship from Spain and struck Marseilles in 588 CE. Ancient records provide information on plague outbreaks that occurred around the world. Arabic writings from as early as the mid-600s referenced the plague. One Irish history records a disease that resembles plague occurring in the British Isles in 664. Theophanes, a Greek writer, claimed there was another outbreak in Constantinople in 747 that devastated the city and surrounding regions.

The Pattern

The outbreaks of plague tended to follow a pattern. First a ship, having picked up plague in another land, put into port. Infected rats came ashore and died. The fleas on the rats fled to new rodent hosts. Weeks or months passed. Infected fleas bit humans, infecting them with the disease. A few people died, then more, then more. Plague eventually broke out on a large scale. For the most part, these types of ship-borne epidemics tended not to spread far inland. In fact, by 750, plague outbreaks had ceased completely. For almost five centuries, there was no sign of plague. But it would return again.

Constantinople was a busy city during the sixth century.

A caravan on the Silk Road

THE BLACK DEATH BEGINS

rade between Europe and Asia had begun
in ancient times. However, it was not always
smooth. Unstable governments made it difficult
to maintain markets and customers. The presence
of raiders over the Asian steppe often made the

overland route too hazardous for business. Even in peaceful times, shipwrecks at sea and natural disasters on land threatened merchants and their cargoes every step of the way.

THE SILK ROAD

By the 1300s, merchants moving valuable silk and other exotic products traveled the Silk Road, a number of connected trade routes on both land and sea. The Silk Road stretched from Luoyang, capital of China's Han Dynasty, to Rome and into Europe. Sea routes extended the Silk Road as far east as modern Indonesia and as far south as Ethiopia and Yemen.

Trade on the Silk Road increased as the route became more stable and safe. The Silk Road trade, however, brought together disease pools. People from far-flung parts of the world had frequent contact. Ships and caravans carried pathogens great distances in fairly short periods of time. More and more, human populations faced diseases strange to them.

The Empty City

Demetrios Kydones, a scholar in Constantinople, witnessed the Black Death epidemic in his city. "Every day we bring out our friends for burial," he wrote. "[E]very day the city becomes emptier and the number of graves increases. . . . Men inhumanely shun each other's company. Fathers do not dare to bury their own sons; sons do not perform . . . last duties to their fathers."[1]

PLAGUE MOVES WEST

Natural disasters may have helped revive the plague. Chinese records from the early fourteenth century mention floods, locust swarms, and even an earthquake that collapsed a mountain. A shift in climate patterns brought drought to a large part of central Asia. Stresses related to environment and climate can drive animals to migrate in search of food and water. In Asia, plague-carrying marmots, gerbils, and other species suddenly may have sought out new habitats. Rodents from isolated areas may have invaded the ecosystems along

Silk

Strong, light, and able to hold vividly colored dyes, silk was a luxury in the Middle Ages. The fiber came from cocoons spun by the domesticated silkworm, the caterpillar of the moth species *Bombyx mori*. People in parts of China began harvesting silkworm cocoons for silk more than 5,000 years ago. The process was a long-held secret. China's emperors decreed death for anyone trying to take silkworms or silkworm eggs to other countries. China's rulers often bribed rivals with silk to keep peace.

By Justinian's time in the sixth century, silk was one of the Byzantine Empire's essential imports. However, the silk trade created some problems. Justinian's Persian rivals made tremendous amounts of money marking up the price of silk that arrived from China. But by then the Chinese were losing their monopoly on silk. The Japanese had smuggled silkworm eggs out of China around 300 CE. In the 550s, Justinian sent spies to China for the same purpose. Legend says that two monks returned with silkworm eggs hidden in bamboo staffs. During the Middle Ages, silk manufacturing spread through the Islamic world and Europe.

the Silk Road. The rodents already there, meanwhile, probably had steady contact with the camel caravans hauling goods—and with the merchants and workers coming from faraway disease pools.

No one knows exactly when or how *Y. pestis* joined the Silk Road caravans. But in 1338, something brought death to the people around Lake Issyk Kul, in what is today Kyrgyzstan. Nestorian Christians maintained the area as a stop on the trade routes. Archaeologists studying the Nestorians' cemetery noted that usually four people died, on average, per year. However, between 1338 and 1339, as many as 100 people died. Some of the gravestones made it clear that disease had killed the person. Experts note that marmots were part of the local ecosystem around Lake Issyk Kul. Guided by these clues, scientists believe plague struck the Nestorian community. Then, the

Fast-Moving Disease

Many diseases move slowly. Plague did, too, at least at first. Part of the reason for the slow advance may be that the plague moved west from Asia only as fast as migrating rodents could take *Y. pestis* into new ecosystems.

By contrast, a disease that circulates in human populations can move very quickly. New strains of influenza, for example, move around the entire world in a year. One of the many mysterious things about the Black Death is that it began to move so far so fast once it reached the Black Sea. Plague in modern times travels between 3 and 20 miles (5 and 32 km) per year. But only 18 months after the Kaffa outbreak, the disease had already reached Sicily, Egypt, Persia, and port cities across southern Europe. It later crossed most of France in just six months.

Plague was carried over water on ships.

disease was likely carried to and from the region on merchant caravans.

For the next six years, plague crept across central Asia. In 1345, it arrived in Sarai. Goods brought from Asia passed through Sarai on the way to Italian merchant colonies on the Black Sea. From there, the fleets of Italian city-states such as Genoa and Venice carried goods to markets in the Mediterranean and Europe.

Genoa had leased the city of Kaffa (now called Feodosia) from the local Mongols, who were called the Tartars by Europeans. Plague arrived in Kaffa in

1346 as the Tartars, angered by a local dispute, laid siege to the Genoese. An account of the time explained:

> *All medical advice and attention was useless, the Tartars died as soon as the signs of the disease appeared on their bodies; swelling in the armpit or groin caused by coagulating humors; followed by a putrid fever.*[2]

The dying and diseased Tartars broke off the siege. They were horrified by the disaster upon them. Reportedly, they used catapults to hurl their dead over the city walls. An Italian official, Gabriele de Mussi, wrote, "What seemed like mountains of dead were thrown into the city."[3] However, De Mussi lived in Piacenza, a town north of Genoa and far away from Kaffa. Historians can only speculate whether or not De Mussi heard the details from merchants and sailors who had witnessed what happened or wrote

Gabriele de Mussi's Story

Most scholars question De Mussi's story regarding the events at Kaffa. Part of the doubt relates to the fact he reported on the events from far away. Science also undermines his version.

Most experts do not believe the bodies catapulted into Kaffa could have caused plague to break out. Since bubonic plague is not contagious, it would not spread from corpses to living people. Even if the bodies had carried pneumonic plague, it is considered unlikely the bacteria would have transferred from a corpse to a living person. While humans have caught plague from dead animals, the infection usually occurs when the person opens up the animal's body for examination. Historians today tend to believe plague reached Kaffa the usual way— by rats. These historians suggest the rats crossed from the Mongol side into the city.

on the basis of unreliable rumors. However, experts do accept that ships probably carried plague south to Constantinople. What future historians called the Black Death had come to the Mediterranean.

Death in the Middle East

The Byzantine capital was no longer the trade and military powerhouse of earlier centuries. But it remained an important market for merchants as well as home to as many as 250,000 people. In 1347, almost eight centuries after Justinian's Plague, the disease returned to the city. How many died is unknown. But all accounts agree that plague devastated the population.

Constantinople served as a gateway to the lands of the Near East and Egypt. Some time in the late summer of 1347, plague reached the island of Cyprus. A ship that docked there late in the year found no one alive and fled. The disease was carried to Alexandria about this same time. By spring of 1348, the plague had followed the Nile River to Cairo. The dying was horrendous. Piles of corpses filled mosques. Without enough coffins and burial shrouds, the city was forced to throw bodies into pits and trenches.

The Black Death was rampant in Egypt's interior through 1348 and 1349. The death toll was unimaginable. Records show that only 116 people in the village of Asyut paid their taxes. Before the plague, 6,000 taxpayers had lived there. So many people died in rural areas that unpicked fruit rotted on trees and crops withered in the ground. Food shipments ceased.

As a child, Arab historian Ibn Kaldun saw the Black Death at work in Tunis, a city in North Africa:

> *Civilization both in the East and the West was visited by a destructive plague which devastated nations and caused populations to vanish. It swallowed up many of the good things of civilization and wiped them out. . . . Cities and buildings were laid waste, roads and way signs obliterated, settlements and mansions became empty. . . . The entire inhabited world changed.*[4]

Islam and Disease

Muslims, like European Christians later, turned to their faith for ways to understand what was happening. Islam had three major views on epidemics. First, it viewed disease as the work of Allah and stated that plague could not be contagious. Second, Muslims dying of plague were admitted to heaven. Finally, Islamic law ordered Muslims to stay out of infected areas and for those already in an infected area to stay there. Not all Muslims agreed with these views or followed the laws, of course. Accounts make it clear the rich and powerful as well as the poor ran from plague.

The plague did not stop in the Middle East. Even as the Black Death swept the Islamic world, it was unleashing catastrophe in Europe. ⌐

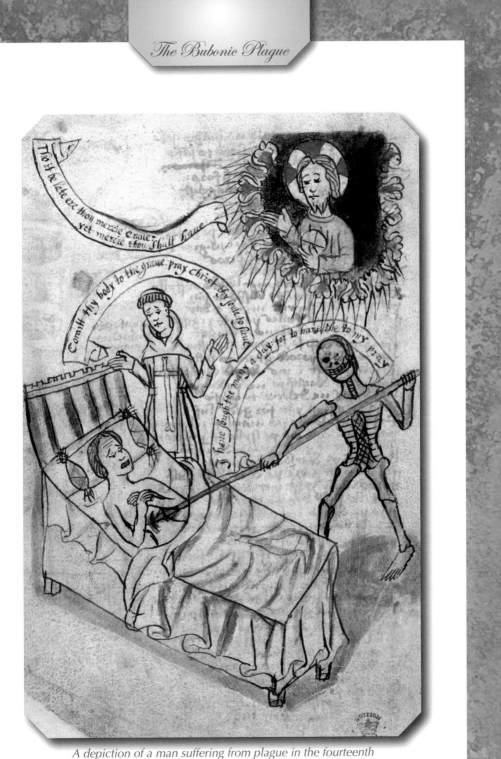

A depiction of a man suffering from plague in the fourteenth
or fifteenth century by an unknown European artist

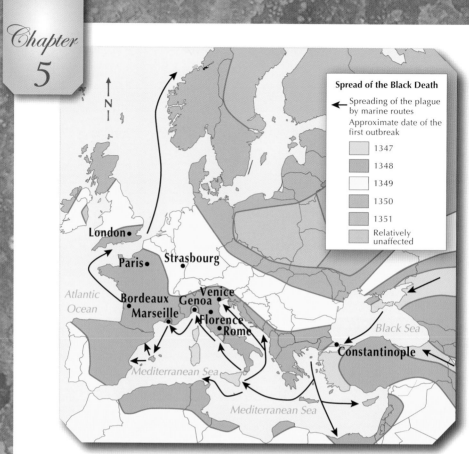

The Black Death was the beginning
of what is known as the Second Pandemic.

EUROPE INVADED

*I*n October 1347, Michael of Piazza, an
Italian friar, reported that a fleet of ships
bound for Genoa stopped over at Messina, Sicily. All
seemed well at first. But a deadly illness swept the city
a short time after the sailors put ashore.

Messina's authorities forced the Genoese ships to leave, but it was already too late. The skyrocketing number of deaths threw the city into a panic. People ran to the countryside to escape. By November, the Black Death had broken out across the island. Sick refugees in Catania received care at a local hospital until the Catanians realized the seriousness of the disease and chased them out of town. The scene in Messina resembled that in Cairo with bodies everywhere and houses deserted.

As ships continued to dock at and leave Sicily, the disease traveled along established trade routes. It most likely spread to Tunis, North Africa, and several Mediterranean islands from Sicily's ships. It may have reached Spain the same way.

CATASTROPHE IN ITALY

The Genoese also carried plague home with them. Personal accounts of the time noted that ships had sailed from Messina to Genoa in the fall. Upon being refused permission to land, three ships continued west. One ship may have infected Marseilles, France's main Mediterranean port. But more plague-carrying ships arrived off Genoa at the end of the year. The Genoese drove them away with flaming arrows. Still, the disease made its way into the city.

Plague had already been carried farther south. It cut through Pisa, and headed inland. Florence and Siena, two of Italy's richest cities, lay in its path. At the time, central Italy had already been hit hard by other misfortunes. Since 1345, too much rain had delayed or ruined crops. Hunger and malnutrition were ongoing problems. Not long before the Black Death arrived, earthquakes shook the region and a banking crisis battered Florence's economy.

A Long Emergency

Europe underwent major changes in the High Middle Ages (1000–1300). Improvements in plows and windmills boosted food supplies. The climate entered a warm phase that opened up new farmland and increased the length of the growing season. People in many places were healthier, richer, and safer than their ancestors. As a result of these and other changes, Europe's population tripled.

Sometime in the late 1200s, however, the climate turned colder and rainier. Floods washed away some crops; cold snaps killed others. Too much rain rotted some plants, and the lack of sunlight stunted their growth. Famine became an ongoing threat. In 1270, the population began to decline. From 1300 to 1320, much of northern Europe experienced one or more famines. Hunger and poverty led to crime and unrest.

Disease, aided by hunger and stress, increased. Human epidemics such as typhoid and dysentery returned. The epidemics, famines, and economic problems continued into the 1340s. With the arrival of the Black Death, many people were already unhealthy, stressed, and vulnerable to disease.

Plague entered the anxious and hungry city of Florence in late winter or early spring. It may have killed half of Florence's 100,000 people. Grave diggers could not keep up with the dead. Corpses were layered in pits. Such treatment shocked Florentines. Their custom was to lay the dead to rest in their church cemetery among relatives and ancestors. To be thrown into a hole with strangers, exposed to weather and animals, was a horrifying concept.

Siena, to the south, was not spared. By early spring, businesses had shut down. Farmers quit coming in from the country. Men still working in the city labored on the local cathedral. The Black Death arrived in mid-April or May. In June, the government shut down and workers began to dig burial pits. Plague had caused more deaths in Siena than it had in Florence. Researchers suggest 50 to 60 percent

The Grave Diggers

With so many dead, the authorities in Florence recruited men from the country and the poorer classes to dispose of the bodies. Soon gangs of shovel-wielding grave diggers known as the *becchini* stalked the streets. The becchini demanded high wages to bury loved ones in the cemeteries of their local churches. Often, though, they tossed the bodies into the nearest graveyard. With the high mortality rate, there were fewer people working in jobs such as grave digging, so the becchini could charge more for their services despite their disrespectful behavior. Their off-duty habits offended people even more. As thousands of Florentines mourned friends and loved ones, the becchini showed off by laughing, drinking, and assaulting innocent people. By summer, becchini gangs were breaking into houses. Those inside had a choice. Pay up or be murdered and declared another plague victim.

of the people in Siena and the surrounding area died.

FROM MARSEILLES TO RUSSIA

Farther west, the Black Death took its toll in Marseilles. The city was one of the Mediterranean's busiest ports. Countless products—including Indian pepper, ivory, and even human slaves—passed through its docks and warehouses. As a trade center, it attracted visitors and workers from far and wide. Beginning in January 1348, those who journeyed to Marseilles encountered a city infected with the Black Death. Others carried the disease in all directions as they fled or moved on with their merchandise. Soon it reached the major cities of southern France. As winter settled in, plague menaced Chauliac in Avignon.

Rural areas began to suffer too. Tax records and other documents suggest nearly half the people died in the rich Languedoc province. As in Egypt, agriculture collapsed. Entire villages were deserted. Valuable

"Breath spread the infection among those speaking together, with one infecting the other, and it seemed as if the victim was struck all at once by the affliction and was, so to speak, shattered by it. This impact . . . so infected and invaded the body that the victims violently coughed up blood and after three days' incessant vomiting, they died."[1]

—Michael of Piazza, providing details that led experts to believe that pneumonic plague struck Sicily

Nuns cared for the sick at Hotel Dieu in Paris, France.

farmland was empty because no one was left to work it. By summer, the Black Death ravaged northern France. Paris may have lost 800 people per day on the worst days. At the main hospital in Paris, the Hotel Dieu, plague killed hundreds of patients every day and the nuns who cared for the sick.

The Black Death moved north in spectacular fashion. In 1348, the English controlled Bordeaux, one of the French provinces on the Atlantic Ocean. Ships from the region, perhaps carrying soldiers or the famous Bordeaux wines, unknowingly transported a darker cargo to England. Soon other ships had landed the Black Death from Plymouth north to Bristol and east to Southampton. "Then this cruel death spread on all sides, following the course of the sun," wrote Henry Knighton, a canon in Leicester.[2] By fall, the plague arrived in London by land and sea.

In northern cities, the Black Death often started as bubonic plague. But the cold and wet winter weather encouraged pneumonic cases, just as it did with influenza and other diseases of the lungs. By the following spring, 2,000 people had been buried in just one London cemetery. Parliament refused to meet in the autumn of 1349. Between one-third and one-half of Londoners perished. It took more than 150 years for the city to return to its pre-Black Death population.

No place in England, however, suffered a higher percentage of lives lost than East Anglia. A wool-producing region surrounded by swamps and water, East Anglia had much of its contact with the outside world through shipping. The Black Death most likely arrived first from continental Europe and later from English cities. Records show that losses in the hardest-hit villages rose to seven deaths out of every ten people. In Norwich, the largest city, half the clergy died. The Black Death was carried north into Scotland and west to Ireland. Throughout 1349 and 1350, it struck the British Isles.

English ships may have carried the disease to the trading town of Bergen, Norway. Within a year, the Black Death had swept Scandinavia. Across the North Sea, it blazed through Holland to the German-speaking lands of Central Europe, into Eastern Europe, and finally to Russia in 1350. By then, the catastrophe had eased in the Mediterranean.

The plague had not followed the shortest route to Russia from Great Sarai northwest into Russian-speaking kingdoms to the north. But there was little contact at the time between the two lands. Instead, the Black Death followed the trade routes across Europe and then boomeranged east.

Modern experts believe that bubonic plague was just one of the three forms of plague that fed into the Black Death. Writers of the time described bubonic and pneumonic plague. The pneumonic plague, in

Near Miss

A few regions of Europe escaped the Black Death. The largest area stretched from what is modern-day eastern Germany through central Poland to Ukraine. No one is sure why these areas did not experience the disease. Black Death also spared a small part of north-ern Spain, a region in Belgium, and scattered communities in Italy's northern mountains.

particular, helps explain the high death tolls. The pneumonic plague kills faster than the bubonic form. Numerous stories tell of victims dying a short time after showing symptoms—or without showing symptoms at all. Since septicemic plague acted even faster than the pneumonic kind, it is probable it also appeared at times.

By 1352, the Black Death had burned itself out in Europe and around the Mediterranean—if only for the time being. Most sources suggest that one-third of Europe's population died. Experts usually apply the same statistic to the Islamic lands. But no one knows how many the Black Death really killed. Countries did not keep population records at the time.

Millions of survivors, however, sensed the enormity of what had happened just by looking at homes empty of loved ones, at Florence's deserted streets, and East Anglia's abandoned villages. Churches were half full during worship and the marketplaces were closed. The unused merchant ships were moored at the docks, and the great burial pits scarred the towns and cities. For the survivors, the Black Death was an unthinkable catastrophe, a personal tragedy, and perhaps, seemingly, the end of their world. ⌐

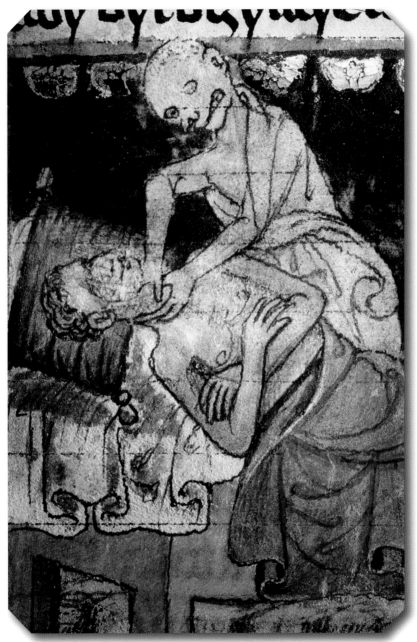

In this 1376 artwork, death is represented as a person, strangling a plague victim.

A scene from the Old Testament shows the release of the plague of boils.

"THE QUIVERING SPEAR
OF THE ALMIGHTY"

city wracked by the Black Death staggered the senses of those who survived. Black flags hung from steeples to warn travelers away. Bodies rotted in the street. Church bells rang continually to mark the passing of lives.

Some mourned lost friends or relatives. Others suffered as surgeons cut open the painful buboes.

TRYING TO UNDERSTAND

In the wake of the astonishing tragedy, people tried to understand how the Black Death could happen. Some Christians believed that God had sent the Black Death to punish those who disobeyed religious teachings. The Old Testament taught that God had used disease against sinners. With this in mind, Gabriele de Mussi, called the plague, "[T]he quivering spear of the Almighty, in the form of plague."[1]

Some priests inclined to believe in God's wrath announced that their parishioners deserved punishment for sinful behavior. Some writers obsessed with morals considered the Black Death a useful hammer against all the things—important or otherwise—that offended them.

Life Goes On

Everyday life continued in many places even as the Black Death raged at its worst. Documents show businessmen in Marseilles made deals. Ordinary people in France and Italy married. English farmers plowed their fields. Ships, though fewer than before, carried on trade. Crime went on too. Lawyers in Florence skimmed fortunes from inheritances created by the plague.

The disaster of the Black Death even failed to stop war. On the Iberian Peninsula, the Christians of Castile warred with the Islamic Moors, a continuation of a series of religious wars that had gone on since the seventh century. When the Black Death hit the Moorish armies in 1349, the Moors considered switching religions to appease the Christian god—until the Castilians caught it too.

Henry Knighton, for example, disliked current women's fashions. Plague, he explained, was a "marvellous remedy" for the problem.[2]

But most people had no interest in philosophy or lectures. For them, the Black Death was a personal tragedy. Millions lost friends and loved ones. "Where are our sweet friends now?" Petrarch asked, writing about 1348. "Where are the beloved faces? Where are the agreeable words, where the soothing and pleasant conversation? . . . Once we were all together, now we are quite alone."[3] Families were left in tatters. "Fathers abandoned their sons, wives their husbands, and one brother the other," Agnolo di Tura of Siena said. "In the end, everyone escapes and abandons anyone who might be infected."[4]

In many cities, morality began to break down. Fleeing nobles and government officials abandoned their responsibilities. The Catholic Church was harshly criticized for its general response to the Black Death. Some Church officials and ordinary priests fled from plague with nobles and government officials. However, historians give Pope Clement credit for trying to stop panic and violence in Avignon and elsewhere. He ordered physicians such as Chauliac to help the sick. Additionally, many priests, monks, and nuns cared for those in need and died of plague beside them.

The Church's image suffered even more because it provided the training for most physicians—and medicine could do nothing to prevent plague or cure someone. "Every pronounced case of plague is incurable," said the physician Chalin de Vinario.[5]

MEDICAL ATTENTION

Medieval medicine's flaws grew out of what physicians considered fact. Medical schools taught a system developed by the Roman philosopher-physician Galen (born approximately in 129 CE). Galen, in turn, borrowed from ideas laid down by the Greeks 500 years earlier.

Galenic medicine believed four so-called humors—blood, phlegm, yellow bile, and black bile—regulated the body. If the humors were out of balance, sickness occurred. Physicians then worked to restore the balance necessary for good health. For example, a physician might bleed

Bad Reputation

The Catholic Church had struggled with its image long before the Black Death. Some cardinals had children, some clergymen were interested only in making money, and some Church leaders gave the best jobs to their relatives. A great many Europeans saw the Church leaders interested in everything but spiritual matters. Pope Clement hardly set a good example. Everyone was aware that he liked women, nice clothes, big meals, and betting on greyhounds.

a patient to bring the humors into balance. Another false belief that influenced thinking about plague involved odors. Since ancient times, Europeans and Middle Easterners had believed a foul-smelling gas or mist called miasma brought disease. Miasma rose from swamps, the sea, and from cracks opened by earthquakes. Astrological forces also created it. The widespread idea of infectious bad air created by dead bodies, sewage, and other decay was related to the miasma theory.

Cities knew that keeping plague away was the best defense. In Milan, both the authorities and private citizens walled up the sick inside their homes. This cruel strategy should not have worked. People may have spread pneumonic plague, but bricks walls in homes did nothing to stop the rats carrying the bubonic form of the disease. Yet Milan had one of the lowest death rates for a European city.

The situation was different elsewhere in Italy. Venice was Europe's richest trading empire. The ships of Venice, like those of Genoa, constantly sailed to and from Black Sea ports. One or more brought plague back in late 1347 about the time the plague reached Sicily. Venice had one of the few public health systems that existed in Europe, and it sprang into action. The main defense was quarantine—keeping the sick isolated from others. Venetian authorities quarantined every ship, along with its crew and cargo, on an island for up to 40 days. Those caught disobeying quarantine faced the death penalty.

Inside the city, the government passed laws stating that any plague case must be reported. Guards kept the sick inside their homes. Barges carried those who died to burial islands. Workers burned clothes, linen, and other personal items belonging to the

Ordinary Filth

Most European cities were dirty beyond belief. As indoor toilets did not exist, everyone used chamber pots. Whenever necessary, a person hollered out the window to look out below and emptied the waste onto the street. Often it lay there with the droppings of wandering livestock.

City dwellers dealt with more than human waste, however. Dead animals rotted where they dropped. Butchers working in the open air flung intestines and other unwanted parts into the street. Surgeons tossed blood and bodily fluids into the gutter.

It did not help that bathing was very uncommon. People generally bathed once a year or less. Lice and the human flea *Pulex irritans* flocked to these filthy human bodies. Skin diseases were epidemic. The only exceptions were those living in the few cities such as Nuremburg in Germany that maintained public baths and encouraged people to use them.

The unsanitary conditions probably aided the Black Death. Not only did the filth attract rats, it also bred other illnesses. Europeans battered for years by ordinary diseases may have had immune systems too weak to fight off plague.

deceased. But quarantine, in Venice at least, failed. Over the next 18 months, an incredible six in ten Venetians—between 72,000 and 90,000 people—may have died.

Other authorities chose to address sin to turn away plague. In Tournai, France, officials ordered all couples living together to get married. It also became illegal to swear. Authorities in Speyer, Germany, banned gambling in the churchyard. King Magnus of Sweden, hoping to ease God's wrath, asked his subjects to walk barefoot to church and to eat only bread and water on Fridays.

Not all reactions to the Black Death were so harmless, however. As plague bored into Europe's interior, some of those in its path looked for someone to blame. Attention settled on the people Christians had scapegoated for centuries: the Jews.

Artwork from the fourteenth century depicts the common practice of bleeding a patient to restore the balance of his humors.

Fifteenth-century Jews having a Passover meal

BLAME AND VIOLENCE

urope's Christians had a long history of blaming Jewish people for misfortune. In part, their animosity came from religious tradition. Jews, in the view of many Christians, were responsible for the death of Christ. Social forces, in particular money, also contributed to the negative feeling. Laws in much of Europe prevented Christians from charging interest for loans. But people still needed credit to start businesses, pay bills, and so on. Since laws barred Jews from most jobs and from owning land, money lending was one of the few businesses open to them. As non-Christians, they could legally make loans and charge interest. But people resented them, especially when payments came due.

Traditionally, violence against the Jewish community peaked during Holy Week, the period between Palm Sunday and Easter. In 1348, Holy Week arrived as the Black Death reached a lethal phase in parts of southern Europe. On Palm Sunday, a Christian mob in the French town of Toulon killed 40 Jews and hung the bodies in the town square. During the attack, townspeople dragged Jews into the streets to spit

Plague Maiden

The legend of the *Pest Jungfrau,* or "plague maiden," arose in German-speaking regions as an explanation for plague. According to the story, the Pest Jungfrau flew from place to place spreading the disease. Often she appeared as a blue flame. It was said the same blue flame flew out of the mouth of dead plague victims. The Pest Jungfrau could also aim the disease at an individual by raising her hand. Lithuanians believed the Pest Jungfrau infected her victims by waving a red scarf through a window or a doorway.

on them and beat them. Homes of the Jews were looted and burned; their money was stolen.

Conspiracy Theory

Pope Clement, appalled by what was happening to the Jews, ordered Christians to stop. By then, however, rumors had begun blaming the Jews for the spread of plague. Jewish agents, people claimed, used poison to plant the Black Death in the wells people used for water.

The tales gained credibility in September 1348. Swiss authorities in Chillon arrested Jewish residents. When "put to the question"—the medieval term for torture—a surgeon named Balavignus described a plot led by Rabbi Jacob. According to the surgeon's story, a network of Jewish agents had fanned out across Europe to poison wells with plague. Investigators in Chillon and, later, other towns tortured additional details out of Jewish prisoners.

It did not matter that the confessions were forced and often contradicted one another. The poisoning plot of the well had not made sense. As many pointed out, Jewish people died of the Black Death as did others. Why would Jews mix a poison that killed their own people?

By the fall of 1348, the fear churned up by the Black Death made people willing to believe anything. Spaniards attacked Jews almost as soon as the Black Death showed itself in their lands. Throughout eastern France, rioters threw Jewish neighbors down wells or burned them at the stake. In the French city of Strasbourg, the Jewish community was marched naked to an open pit for execution. Enraged citizens in Basel on the Rhine River in Switzerland herded the towns' Jews into a single building and burned them alive. In Esslingen,

Anti-Semitism

A hatred of Jewish people had a long history in Europe. It intensified in the 1100s when the blood libel became a part of Christian belief and European culture. The blood libel referred to the belief that Jewish people murdered Christian children and used their blood for dark purposes.

Over the next two centuries, Christians adopted many anti-Jewish stories and stereotypes. Anti-Semitic incidents became more common. In 1240, the French authorities put the Talmud, an important Jewish work, on trial. They later accused Jews of plotting with Muslims to conquer Christian Europe. Violence during Holy Week was a frequent occurrence.

Attacks on Jewish communities, called pogroms, occurred from the twelfth century onward. The authorities made it easy for angry mobs to find targets. In many places, Jewish people had to wear special markers on their clothes. English Jews wore strips of cloth on the chest; French Jews wore a yellow patch. Jews in Poland wore pointed green hats. A long tradition of considering Jews outsiders and killers, as well as resentment for their charging interest for loans, helped pave the way for the violence of the Black Death years.

A woodcut from 1493 of flagellants

a mob sealed Jews inside a synagogue and set the building on fire.

RISE OF THE FLAGELLANTS

Terror of the Black Death and the fear of God's wrath stirred religious fanaticism as well as hatred. Flagellant cults dated back to the 1260s. These men, inspired by Christ's example, whipped themselves to gain forgiveness for their sins and for those of other people. Over the years, flagellant groups came and went. But the catastrophe unleashed by the Black Death created a flagellant movement different from those that had come before in that it was bigger, more widespread, and more violent.

The flagellants during the Black Death years belonged to organized groups. The men included nobles, craftsmen, merchants, and others able to pay the entrance fee to the master. The fee, though small, kept the poor from joining, since those without the money could not participate. How the money was used and how the bands recruited followers is unclear. An individual joined only after he confessed all of the sins he had ever committed. In addition, he agreed to pay his own expenses and accept no charity.

Dancing Mania

The behavior of the flagellants was not the only strange reaction to plague. In 1374, during a later occurrence of plague, several cities along the Rhine River broke out in an epidemic of dancing. Supernatural forces were said to be at work. "[W]hile dancing they sang and [said] the names of unheard-of devils," said Radulfus de Rivo. "When the dance was over the devils tormented them with violent pains in their chests."[1] Priests in the city of Liege were famous for driving the demons out of dancers.

Other dancing manias were believed to have more earthly causes. During plague epidemics in Germany, people in Munich and elsewhere willingly gathered together to dance to keep up their spirits in a dark time.

The flagellants announced their approach to a town by singing hymns. As they neared, townspeople crowded the public square and church bells rang. Inside the local church, each flagellant stripped to the waist and struck his body with a three-pronged whip. Then, the entire band collapsed to the floor. Each flagellant lay in a way that expressed his worst sin. As the master walked by, he struck the flagellant with a spiked lash.

Afterward, the main part of the ritual began. The flagellants stood in a circle. Three of the members stepped into the middle of the circle and screamed at the others to whip themselves harder and faster. The flagellants tried to outdo one another in punishment. The master finished by reading a letter in which God vowed to destroy the world with disease and other disasters if human beings continued to sin.

Flagellants took time out from their own performances to provoke mob violence against Jewish communities. In Germany, flagellants often (though not always) played a role in sparking attacks, called pogroms, on Jewish communities. In 1349, a flagellant-led rampage wiped out the entire Jewish population of Brussels, Belgium.

CHALLENGING THE CHURCH

As time went on, flagellants began to challenge the Church. Like many Europeans at the time, they saw its officials as some of the worst sinners of all. Flagellants ridiculed Church beliefs. Some referred to priests as thieves and bloodsuckers. In a few cases, flagellants attacked clergymen. Eventually, the most ambitious flagellant masters tried to seize Church powers and wealth for themselves.

Pope Clement retaliated by ordering his officials to root out flagellant supporters in the Church. He also asked kings and other leaders to suppress the flagellant movement. Authorities in many places, weary of the violence, banned marches and executed members of the bands. Clement declared the flagellants' beliefs to be in violation of the teachings of the Church. By the end of 1350, the flagellant movement

Flagellant Vows

Each flagellant in a band, regardless of rank, obeyed a list of strict rules. First and foremost, a flagellant promised to whip his body twice in public and once in private every day. They could not wash, shave, or change their clothes. Except for prayers and singing, they remained silent—unless the band's leader, the master or father, gave them permission to speak. Contact with women was also forbidden.

had fallen apart. Their strange and violent time had lasted less than two years. Their rise to prominence had been a result of the extreme conditions created by plague.

Flagellants arrived in a town during their pilgrimage.

Plague victims in Paris in 1544

THE SECOND PANDEMIC

By 1352, the Black Death had left behind millions of grief-stricken and traumatized people who tried to make sense of what had happened. If God had sent plague to punish the wicked, as some believed, many people ignored the lesson. Writers of the time noted how people threw themselves into eating well and often, drinking the best wines, gambling, holding parties, and hanging out in taverns. The survivors, it seems, were determined to enjoy life. However, the Black Death was only the beginning of the Second Pandemic, which would last for more than four centuries.

A SHIFT IN POWER

The Church was unable to put a stop to sinning. Many surviving clergymen, having deserted their followers for fear of plague, returned to find people insulted them as they walked down the street. Pope Clement was just as critical. "[A]bout what can you preach to the people?" he asked. "If on humility, you yourselves are the proudest in the world. . . . If on poverty, you are the most grasping and most covetous."[1]

Celebrating Life

Fashion was a popular way to express the new love for life. Women enjoyed eye-popping wigs, brightly colored low-necked tops, and tight skirts. Men's fashions included a short coat that clung to the body—an early version of the modern jacket. Shoes also made a statement. During the Black Death, the morally minded had blamed plague in part on God's disapproval of pointed shoes. In a post-plague society, pointed shoes became the thing to wear.

Nobles and landowners also faced new attitudes. In western Europe, laws had once tied farmers to their lands. The Black Death had killed so many workers that the old system no longer worked. Survivors now had their choice of jobs. Landowners had no alternative. If they did not offer more money, lower rent, and better treatment, the farmers simply walked away from the crops and livestock to take a job elsewhere. A great many rural people gave up country life altogether. With their reduced populations, cities offered new job opportunities. Employers, desperate for workers, paid higher wages than ever before to attract employees.

PLAGUE RETURNS

Even though the Black Death had ended, new plague epidemics hit Europe. In the early 1360, the *Pestis Secundus* (Second Plague) wiped out more lives in some areas than

the Black Death had a decade earlier. The Second
Plague was one of the worst disease catastrophes in
history. Estimates suggest that one in five people
died in England. Places as far apart as Florence and
Normandy suffered similar losses.

Plague remained a frequent visitor to Europe
and the Middle East for more than four centuries.
Although most historical attention is given to the
first epidemic, the Black Death, most European and
Near Eastern generations in the four centuries to
follow experienced plague. Every four to five years,
or sometimes every ten to twelve years, the disease
returned. It was almost always bubonic. Usually it
appeared in the summer when temperatures were
warm enough for the Oriental rat flea to move
around.

Galenic medicine still had no answers to the
disease. But some governments did try to better
manage outbreaks. Venice and Florence, for
example, kept up the quarantine systems that isolated
ships suspected of carrying plague. On land, public
health workers took charge of special hospitals called
lazarettos, or "pesthouses."

Lazarettos had little in common with modern
hospitals. Authorities used the buildings to lock up

Worries about miasma
lay at the heart of much
medical advice. Experts
recommended people
use pleasant odors to can-
cel out bad air. European
and Islamic authorities
alike agreed that burning
strong-scented woods,
such as juniper and ash,
and the leaves of orange
and lemon trees foiled
disease. Sulfur, though
far less pleasant, also did
the job. Others created
healing fumes by pouring
oils from herbs onto hot
bricks.

By the seventeenth
century, physicians in
Marseilles dressed in wax-
covered cloth and wore
masks with large beaks.
The mixture of strong-
smelling spices and herbs
in the beak was supposed
to protect the "beak doc-
tors" from bad air.

plague victims—not to heal them.
Attendants abused or ignored
patients while the sick wandered
the halls screaming in agony. After
visiting a Bologna pesthouse in 1630,
one cardinal wrote:

> *Here you see people lament, others cry,
> others strip themselves to the skin, others
> die, others become black and deformed,
> others lose their minds. Here you are
> overwhelmed by intolerable smells. Here
> you cannot walk but among corpses.*[2]

Other measures were more
humane. During one Spanish
outbreak, the authorities went house
to house trading new mattresses for
old ones. The mattresses were burned
along with dirty linen and clothes.
Some methods made no difference
but seemed sensible at the time. The
government in Tournai, France, for
instance, fired cannons and guns
to break up clouds of miasma they
believed hung over the city.

THE GREAT PLAGUE OF LONDON

In 1663 and 1664, plague raged in Amsterdam and the Scandinavian and German ports. The following year, it crossed the English Channel and unleashed an outbreak of mostly bubonic plague known the Great Plague of London.

The Great Plague began as epidemics usually did in cities— among the poor. Few Londoners paid attention at first. Public health was, in any case, a low priority. As a rule, the local government threw together hasty half-measures whenever plague broke out. Old women, not

The Plague Village

In September 1665, George Viccars, a tailor in the village of Eyam, received an order of cloth from plague-battered London. The cloth, it turned out, contained fleas. Four or five days later, Viccars was dead of bubonic plague. Five other people died within the month. But cool weather arrived. Eyam appeared saved.

In the summer of 1666, as plague roared back, frightened townspeople began to leave town. Local clergyman William Mompasson understood that plague refugees would take the disease with them. To save other towns and the nearby city of Sheffield, Mompasson asked the villagers to remain in quarantine inside Eyam. Most villagers did as he asked. Throughout the summer, the residents of Eyam did whatever was necessary to avoid contact with the outside world. People outside the town brought food and other goods to a stream in exchange for money the villagers left in the water. A local nobleman also donated food.

Still, plague racked the town, and 260 people died. Mompasson's wife was one of them. The clergyman survived and wrote, "The condition of the place has been so sad that I persuade myself it did exceed all history and example."[3]

Comets and War

The London epidemic began at an ominous time. A brilliant comet flared in the night sky starting in November. People had long believed comets foretold disaster. England and Holland were preparing to go to war, but that did not keep English and Dutch merchants from carrying on trade. Aware of plague outbreaks in Holland, Charles II, England's king, ordered quarantine for Dutch ships. Yet government officials, the king included, allowed ships carrying special goods to disobey the law.

health professionals, determined who did and did not have the disease. As London lacked lazarettos, officials boarded up plague victims with their entire families, trapping them in their houses and left them to live or die. Or at least, they tried. People in St. Giles of the Fields, a plague-stricken area near Westminster, rioted rather than allowing it. Barricading people in their houses failed to stop plague since rats simply scuttled past the boards and stones. This method most likely killed healthy people who were not able to escape from their homes.

Plague tore through the city outskirts and moved into the heart of London. The rich and powerful fled. But workers, artisans, and the poor had no choice but to stay and ride out the disaster. As the summer weather took hold, the epidemic grew more serious. Thousands of people took boats on the Thames River to isolate

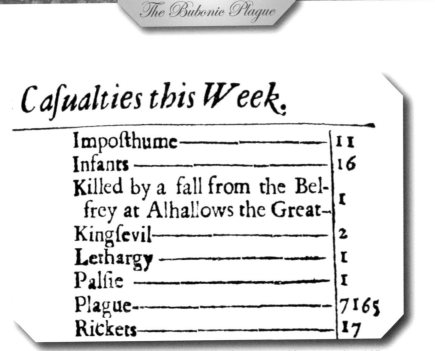

Casualties this Week.

Imposthume	11
Infants	16
Killed by a fall from the Belfrey at Alhallows the Great	1
Kingsevil	2
Lethargy	1
Palsie	1
Plague	7165
Rickets	17

Londoners recorded the number of deaths in a weekly census in 1665.

themselves. Schools, theaters, and most public places closed.

The exact number of people killed in the Great Plague of London is unclear. In 1665, the government claimed 68,596 people had died. The figure was revised upward to 97,000. Modern-day historians suggest at least 100,000 people died.

The Great Plague was London's last widespread epidemic. On September 2, 1666, a fire burned most of the city. In the aftermath, the city rebuilt with stone and brick instead of wood. Tile took the place of thatch as the main material for roofs. Both changes made life more difficult for rats. As the rodents moved outdoors, they took fleas away from potential human hosts.

The Fading Pandemic

Marseilles, France, suffered the last of the city's great epidemics in 1720. Though outbreaks continued in Eastern Europe, the Middle East, and North Africa, plague slowly faded from European history. However, the disease still lurked in its reservoir among the rodents of central Asia. Little more than 100 years after the last European epidemics, plague emerged once more. This time *Y. pestis*, helped by modern travel, spread around the world. ⌁

The Great Plague of London killed at least 100,000 people.

Alexander Yersin was an adventurer and scientist.

A New Era

The Third Pandemic of plague began around 1855 in Yunnan, a province of southwestern China. Whether plague was endemic or came from elsewhere is unknown. From Yunnan, plague followed the trade routes east to Pakhoi in

1877. When the disease arrived in Canton in 1894, it had already cut through a large part of southern China. In that year, the disease traveled from Canton 90 miles (145 km) down the Pearl River to Hong Kong.

OUTBREAK IN HONG KONG

In 1894, Hong Kong was a British colony and one of the world's most important ports. The elite of a few thousand Europeans ruled the colony and controlled its rich trade. A small army of clerks, government officials and workers, supervisors, and others kept business humming along. The business, in turn, depended on 200,000 or more Chinese workers—men, women, and children—who provided cheap labor.

On May 8, 1894, physician James Lowson diagnosed the first-known plague victim in the city. Lowson soon found 20 more cases at one of the inadequate local clinics. Officials moved quickly. Patients suspected of having plague were sent to a ship that served as a floating lazaretto. Inspectors went house to house looking for sick people, had unsanitary buildings knocked down, and supervised the digging of mass graves.

Shibasaburo Kitasato

When plague broke out in Hong Kong in 1894, Shibasaburo Kitasato was one of the world's best-known bacteriologists. Before coming to Hong Kong, he had worked with the harmful bacterium that caused tetanus. Hong Kong's British rulers, pleased to have such an expert on hand, welcomed the Japanese scientist and his team by providing laboratory space and other assistance. For a time, his contributions to the discovery of *Y. pestis* were overlooked, but Kitasato has since been recognized. In later years, he and one of his students made further medical history by finding one of the causes of dysentery—an often fatal disease of the intestine.

The chance to study plague brought a number of scientists to Hong Kong. Two scientists, Shibasaburo Kitasato and the scientist-adventurer Alexander Yersin, shared credit for the discovery of the plague bacteria. Yersin, however, made a second observation that Kitasato overlooked. Seeing dead rats everywhere, Yersin decided to investigate. He found the rats were infected with the same microbe he had found in buboes on human corpses. "Rats," he said, "are certainly the principal propagators of the epidemic."[1] Science had not yet solved the mystery of plague, but Yersin brought it a step closer.

The Hong Kong epidemic had eased by September 1894. Just over 2,500 people died, all but 38 of whom were Chinese. From 1896 to 1929, cases cropped up almost every summer.

Bombay Nightmare

In the late 1890s, trade linked Hong Kong
to India, another British colony. In September
1896, plague turned up in Bombay (Mumbai).
A. G. Viegas, a local physician, found symptoms in
five grain warehouse workers. Though the British
authorities criticized his diagnosis, Viegas was proved
correct.

From late 1896 through the early part of 1897,
almost half of Bombay's citizens fled the city. The
British authorities, overwhelmed by quarantine
and sanitation work, turned to vaccines to stop the
epidemic. Yersin had created a plague vaccine by
injecting plague into horses. By drawing off the
horse's blood, Yersin created a serum he hoped
would boost human immune systems. Officials in
Bombay begged him to bring the still-imperfect
serum to the city. He brought 700 doses and
wished he had 7,000. While in Bombay, he also
treated patients and ventured into slums to further
investigate the disease. About half of those who
received his serum lived. Improvements by colleagues
in Paris made it 80 percent effective.

When Yersin left India, Paul-Louis Simond,
a bacteriologist, took over for him. Simond was

Alexander Yersin

Alexander Yersin, a Swiss-born bacteriologist, was a medical officer in the French Colonial Service and stationed in French Indo-China at the time of the Hong Kong outbreak. He received an order from Paris to go to Hong Kong and use his expertise to try to prevent the spread of the disease. Yersin had trained in laboratories in Europe, including the Pasteur Institute. Excited by the chance to study plague, Yersin set sail for Hong Kong. But, from the start, he bumped up against hardships. He had to work in a straw hut. Kitasato blocked him from examining dead plague victims. But Yersin's tireless laboratory work proved that a bacterium caused bubonic plague. Though Kitasato made similar discoveries, he also made mistakes. The two men shared credit for unlocking the plague bacterium, but *Yersinia pestis* was named for Yersin.

intrigued by the flea bites found on plague victims. From his own investigations, he knew Indians ran away from dead rats. He had also found flea-covered rats in the houses of sick people. He wrote a paper and declared that the flea species *Xenopsylla cheopis* carried plague bacteria from rodents to humans. But the scientific community ignored or dismissed his research. Simond died in 1947 without receiving any credit for his discovery.

Despite advances in knowledge, plague in India broke out again and again. Another rodent carrier, the gray or Norway rat, had made it to the country from northern Asia, adding to a list that already included many native rodents. In the 30 years after 1896, at least 12.5 million Indians died of bubonic (and on rare occasions pneumonic) plague.

HAWAIIAN TRAGEDY

From Bombay and Hong Kong, plague followed shipping routes to New Zealand and Sydney, Australia. In Sydney, officials hired professional rat catchers to exterminate local rodents. Authorities also burned down a slum area known to harbor plague. In all, 103 of 303 plague patients died— slightly more than one in three.

In June 1899, just months before the outbreak in Sydney, plague arrived in Hawaii aboard the merchant ship the *Nippon Miru*. Though authorities sent the ship to the local quarantine island, the rodents aboard made their way to land. Beginning in September, massive numbers of dead rats turned up, especially around Honolulu's Chinatown district. Local health authorities declared a local man dead of plague on December 11. Two days later, the newspapers announced the disease had arrived in Hawaii.

In 1899, Hawaii was a territory of the United States, and a small National Guard unit handled emergencies. Regulations banned travel in and out of Honolulu, and authorities quarantined Chinatown. Guardsmen set up barricades and lines of men around the part of Chinatown under suspicion of harboring infection. The quarantine held in a population that included Chinese, Japanese, and native Hawaiians. Hardship followed for those quarantined. Food ran short. Businesses suffered. Honolulu's shipping slowed because workers were not available to unload cargo.

When plague seemed to disappear, Hawaii's health officials faced criticism that they had done too much. Chinese and Japanese leaders called the quarantine racist. Businessmen wanted to get back to making money. Officials, faced with pressure, lifted the quarantine.

Plague resurfaced by the end of the month. The quarantine went back into effect, and the guardsmen returned to keep it in place. Clifford B. Wood, a physician with the Board of Health, soon went public with a new anti-plague strategy. "[A]ll wooden buildings in which a case of plague occurs, and all wooden buildings [nearby] . . . [would be] burned as soon as possible."[2]

Those inside Chinatown resented the policy. Some of those outside, however, pushed for even more extreme measures when plague killed Sarah Boardman, a suburban woman. Health officials fought off demands to burn all of Chinatown.

Downtown Honolulu in the late nineteenth century

Wood and his colleagues stuck to their original policy. On January 20, 1900, firefighters began a controlled burn of shacks suspected of harboring plague. The controlled burn became an inferno and fire blazed through Chinatown. Volunteers outside of Chinatown rushed in to help residents evacuate. But a large group of armed men also set up a line to prevent residents from leaving for fear they would spread plague. Chinese leaders and government officials, however, managed to calm the situation. The fire left 6,000 people homeless.

PLAGUE ENTERS THE UNITED STATES

Plague arrived in North America in much the same way as it had in Hawaii. The ship, *America*, docked in San Francisco, California, on January 2, 1900. Again, rodents scurried off the boat. Again, bubonic plague cases turned up a couple of months later. And, again, the disease struck the local Chinatown.

In San Francisco, however, health experts had a difficult time getting the authorities to act. Government and business leaders

Plague Bombs

Plague's long history as a biological weapon may have begun with the Mongols at Kaffa in 1346, but it continued on a far greater scale during World War II (1939–1945). At Ping Fan, Manchuria, Japanese microbiologist Shiro Ishii organized a massive laboratory complex and prison that was code-named Unit 731. There, between 3,000 and 4,000 scientists, technicians, and soldiers conducted medical experiments on prisoners they referred to as *murata*, or logs. More than 10,000 Han Chinese and Allied prisoners died as a result of years of brutal and gruesome "studies."

The scientists of Unit 731 considered plague one of the most promising biological weapons. Staffers harvested the deadliest strains of the disease from prisoners. Afterward, technicians grew *Y. pestis* in huge, aluminum vats.

Unit 731 tested several weapons. In 1940, Japanese planes dropped grain coated with plague bacteria above Ningbo, China. In other places, plague-infected fleas were packed into porcelain bulbs and loaded onto bombs. The exploding bombs then scattered fleas across a wide area. Airplanes sometimes sprayed diseased fleas over towns. Staff at Unit 731 even handed out plague-soaked buns to the hungry children of their enemies.

understood that news of a bubonic plague outbreak would hurt the city's reputation. The Chinese community, meanwhile, feared for their jobs and civil rights. Frustrated public health official Joseph Kinyoun took it upon himself to ban all travel for everyone, although the press and the government criticized him. The plague simmered over the next four years. As bubonic plague often did, it eased in winter and surged in summer.

Plague's existence in North America dates from the San Francisco epidemic. The fleas on the city rats found new rodent hosts in the country. Squirrels carried *Y. pestis* into northern California. The bacterium then steadily invaded ecosystem after ecosystem. After a brief outbreak in Los Angeles, California, in 1924, the plague spread eastward across the desert. In a matter of decades, plague circulated in squirrels, marmots, chipmunks, and prairie dogs across the West.

Pneumonic Plague Returns

In the meantime, outbreaks continued in Asia. In 1910 and 1911, pneumonic plague broke out along a railway line in Manchuria. Thousands of people had flocked to the region to make money hunting marmots for fur. Pneumonic plague spread quickly through the crude, crowded hostels where hunters stayed overnight and the trains they traveled on.

Wu Lien-teh, a Malayan bacteriologist-physician educated in Britain, went to Manchuria at the request of the Chinese government. Once there, he experienced numerous obstacles. At one hospital, the staff refused to wear masks despite the fact pneumonic plague spread through the air. Instead, they believed a vaccine developed in India by bacteriologist Waldemar Haffkine would protect them from catching plague. However, the Haffkine vaccine proved inadequate, and many hospital staffers became ill and died. At Wu's urging, masks became more common.

Wu also insisted on burning the dead bodies. Once again, the Chinese resisted. As with mass burial, cremation violated Chinese culture and beliefs. It took an order from the emperor in Peking to give Wu the authority to burn plague victims. Wu later stated the epidemic eased from that point on. But 60,000 people died. Another pneumonic outbreak in 1920 and 1921 killed almost 10,000 people.

MEDICINE AT LAST

Drugs to cure plague remained unknown until antibiotics—a family of drugs that kill bacteria—were discovered in the 1930s and 1940s. Streptomycin, discovered at Rutgers University in 1943, was one of the first medicines that worked against plague. Antibiotics, if given early in the illness, cut bubonic plague's death rate to less than 5 percent. Quick treatment can also save victims of pneumonic and septicemic plague.

A combination of prevention and antibiotics has kept plague in check for most of the past 80 years. As of 2010, more people in the United States were struck by lightning than infected by plague. However, modern plague outbreaks do occur. In 1994, bubonic, and possibly pneumonic, plague hit Surat, the twelfth-largest city in India. According to the World Health Organization (WHO), 54 people died.

Terrorism

In the twenty-first century, the fear of plague in the United States usually does not involve ship rats or sudden outbreaks. It is about terrorism. Plague is considered one of four pathogens—along with smallpox, tularemia, and anthrax—most likely to be used as a biological weapon. Scientists in the former Soviet Union worked on plague weapons. The Soviets called their program *Biopreparat*. It included dozens of laboratories, factories, and testing sites across the country. Scientists turned dried plague bacteria into a powder and placed it in missiles and artillery shells. After the dissolution of the Soviet Union, some Biopreparat scientists claimed they had created plague that could fight off multiple antibiotic drugs.

Plague is an ongoing problem in parts of Africa. The disease reached Madagascar from Bombay in 1898. During the late 1990s, frequent epidemics caused almost 6,000 plague cases. The largest plague outbreaks in recent years have occurred in the war-torn Ituri region of the Democratic Republic of Congo. The pneumonic plague broke out in a diamond-mining area in 2005 and again in the following year.

Poor countries such as Madagascar simply lack access to the antibiotics and public health expertise that have mostly eliminated the disease in wealthy countries. However, as the Third Pandemic continues, a nation's level of wealth may not provide protection from the disease. A future plague epidemic could come about because of an act of war rather than as a natural disaster. A nation or an extremist group could unleash plague on an enemy as a weapon. The danger of a widespread epidemic becomes greater if the attackers have access to a strain of plague that resists antibiotics or quickly evolves into the contagious pneumonic form. Science and understanding tamed plague in the twentieth century. But the threat remains.

Kinyoun's laboratory

Timeline

542–544 CE	588	747
Justinian's Plague, which would turn into the First Pandemic, breaks out in Constantinople and around the Mediterranean Sea.	Plague spreads to Marseilles, France, from Spain.	Constantinople and the surrounding area experience another outbreak of bubonic plague.

1347	1347	1349
The Black Death reaches Constantinople and Cyprus.	The Black Death enters Europe at Messina, Sicily, late in the year.	The flagellant movement peaks.

1320s–early 1330s

The Black Death and the start of the Second Pandemic probably first appears in Mongolia or central Asia.

1338

The Black Death reaches the Nestorian Christian community at Lake Issyk Kul.

1346

The Mongol attack on Kaffa is interrupted by the Black Death epidemic.

1352

The Black Death dies out in Europe and the Mediterranean.

1360s

The Second Plague begins in Europe and elsewhere.

1665

The Great Plague of London occurs.

TIMELINE

1743	1770–1772	1855
The last major plague outbreak occurs in Messina, Sicily.	Plague strikes Moscow in eastern Europe. It is the last major European plague outbreak.	The Third Pandemic of plague begins in China.

1900	1907	1910–1911
Infected ship rats cause a bubonic plague outbreak in San Francisco, California.	San Francisco is hit by a second, larger plague outbreak.	Pneumonic plague devastates Manchuria.

1894

In Hong Kong, Alexander Yersin and Shibasaburo Kitasato separately discover the bacterium that causes plague.

1896

Bubonic plague spreads to India from Hong Kong.

1899

The *Nippon Miru* carries bubonic plague to Honolulu, Hawaii.

1925

The last major US bubonic plague outbreak occurs in Los Angeles, California.

1942

The Japanese army uses plague as a biological weapon in China.

1943

Scientists discover streptomycin, one of the first drugs effective against plague.

ESSENTIAL FACTS

DATE OF EVENT

The first known outbreak occurred in 541 CE.

PLACE OF EVENT

Asia, Europe, the Middle East, North Africa; later worldwide

KEY PLAYERS

- Alexander Yersin
- Pope Clement VI
- Guy de Chauliac
- Kitasato Shibasaburo
- Paul-Louis Simond
- Procopius
- Wu Lien-teh

HIGHLIGHTS OF EVENT

- The plague bacterium *Yersinia pestis* evolved within the last 20,000 years and infected rodents.
- The first known plague epidemic and beginning of the First Pandemic, called Justinian's Plague, appeared in Egypt and Constantinople at the end of 541 CE. It spread to the Middle East, Europe, and Persia.
- The Black Death entered European history in 1346 when it struck a Mongol army attacking the city of Kaffa. Ships from the Italian city of Genoa probably carried it from Kaffa to Constantinople. Over the next year, other ships spread plague. In 1347, the disease reached Messina, Sicily. From there it moved into North

Africa, Spain, and the rest of Europe. This was the start of the Second Pandemic.

❖ No one truly knows how many died in the Black Death, but historians estimate that approximately 25 million people died in Europe (one in three people) and about the same in the Islamic world. The numbers in China, central Asia, and India are less certain.

❖ Plague remained a problem in Europe through the eighteenth century and in the Middle East into the nineteenth century. The period is known as the Second Plague.

❖ The Third Pandemic began in China around 1855. In 1894, plague became an issue in Hong Kong. From there, it spread to India and killed more than 12.5 million Indians over the next 30 years. Plague also broke out in Asia, Africa, Europe, Australia, Hawaii, and in North and South America. As of 2010, plague is carried by rodents on every continent except Australia and Antarctica.

Quote

"None of the earlier epidemics were as severe, since they occupied a single region, while this involved the entire world; the others were curable in some manner, this by none."—*Guy de Chauliac*

Glossary

antibiotic
A type of drug that kills bacteria.

bubo
A swollen lymph node seen in cases of bubonic plague.

endemic
An disease that is always present in an area, even if it is not obvious.

epidemic
A disease that causes more cases than normal in a population.

flagellant
A person who whips himself to make up for his sins or those of others.

immune system
A system of cells and organs that defends the human body against invasion by viruses and bacteria.

lazaretto
A type of hospital once used to isolate and imprison people with plague.

medieval
Belonging to the time period from approximately 470 CE until the fifteenth century. The medieval era is also called the Middle Ages.

pandemic
A disease that has spread across a large part of the world.

pathogen
A virus, bacteria, fungus, or parasite that causes disease. Sometimes referred to as a germ.

quarantine
The practice of isolating sick people from others to keep a disease from spreading.

reservoir
In medicine, a reservoir is a population of animals where a disease always circulates.

steppe
> A grassy, treeless plain with a dry climate.

vector
> An animal or other organism that carries disease from one species to another.

zoonosis
> A disease of animals that crosses over to humans.

ADDITIONAL RESOURCES

SELECTED BIBLIOGRAPHY

Aberth, John. *The Black Death: A Brief History with Documents*. Boston: Bedford/St. Martin's, 2005. Print.

Boccaccio, Giovanni, *The Decameron*. New York: Oxford UP, 1993. Print.

Kelly, John. *The Great Mortality: An Intimate History of the Black Death, the Most Devastating Plague of All Time*. New York: HarperCollins, 2006. Print.

McNeill, William. *Plagues and Peoples*. Garden City, NY: Anchor Press/Doubleday, 1976. Print.

Mohr, James C., *Plague and Fire: Battling Black Death and the 1900 Burning of Honolulu's Chinatown*. New York: Oxford UP, 2005. Print.

FURTHER READINGS

Lynette, Rachel. *Bubonic Plague*. Farmington Hills, MI: KidHaven, 2004. Print.

Slavicek, Louise Chipley. *The Black Death*. New York: Chelsea House, 2008. Print.

Tuchman, Barbara. *A Distant Mirror: The Calamitous Fourteenth Century*. New York: Ballantine, 1987. Print.

Web Links

To learn more about the bubonic plague visit ABDO Publishing Company online at **www.abdopublishing.com**. Web sites about the bubonic plague are featured on our Book Links page. These links are routinely monitored and updated to provide the most current information available.

Places to Visit

Eyam Museum
Hawkhill Road, Eyam, Derbyshire, S32 5QP, United Kingdom
01433-631371
http://www.eyammuseum.demon.co.uk

The Eyam Museum tells the story of how the locals remained in their town rather than flee and carry plague with them. Those interested can walk around the city of Eyam.

Global Health Odyssey Museum
1600 Clifton Road, Atlanta, Georgia 30333
404-639-0830
http://www.cdc.gov/museum/index.htm
The Global Health Odyssey Museum teaches about the Center for Disease Control and Prevention (CDC), public health, and disease prevention.

Source Notes

Chapter 1. Death in Avignon

1. Leo M. Zimmerman and Ilza Veith. *Great Ideas in the History of Surgery*. San Francisco: Norman, 1993. Print. 156.

2. Ibid.

3. John Aberth. *The Black Death: A Brief History with Documents*. Boston: Bedford/St. Martin's, 2005. Print. 66.

Chapter 2. The Adversaries

None.

Chapter 3. Justinian's Plague

1. Procopius. *History of the Wars, Books I and II*. Trans. H. B. Dewing. Cambridge, MA: Harvard UP, 1979. Print. 457.

2. Ibid. 457, 459.

3. Lester K. Little. *Plague and the End of Antiquity: The Pandemic of 541–750*. New York: Cambridge UP, 2007. Print. 7.

Chapter 4. The Black Death Begins

1. John Kelly. *The Great Mortality: An Intimate History of the Black Death, the Most Devastating Plague of All Time.* New York: Harper, 2006. Print. 81.

2. Mark Wheelis. "Biological warfare at the 1346 Siege of Caffa." *Emerging Infectious Diseases* 8. Centers for Disease Control and Prevention, 26 July 2002. Web. 15 Oct. 2010.

3. Ibid.

4. Michael W. Dols. *The Black Death in the Middle East.* Princeton, NJ.: Princeton UP, 1977. Print. 67.

Chapter 5. Europe Invaded

1. Rosemary Horrox, editor. *The Black Death.* Manchester, UK: Manchester UP, 1994. Print. 36.

2. Robert S. Gottfried. *The Black Death: Natural and Human Disaster in Medieval Europe.* New York: Free Press, 1983. Print. 59.

SOURCE NOTES CONTINUED

Chapter 6. "The Quivering Spear of the Almighty"

1. John Aberth. *The Black Death: A Brief History with Documents*. Boston: Bedford/St. Martin's, 2005. Print. 99.

2. Philip Ziegler. *The Black Death*. New York: Harper, 1971. Print. 36.

3. John Aberth. *The Black Death: A Brief History with Documents*. Boston: Bedford/St. Martin's, 2005. Print. 74.

4. Ibid. 81.

5. Johannes Nohl. *The Black Death: A Chronicle of the Plague*. Trans. C. H. Clarke. Yardley, PA: Westholme, 2006. Print. 72.

6. Jonathan Usher. "Franceso Petrarca: Ad Seipsum (To Himself)." *Decameron Web.* n.p., 12 Mar. 2010. Web. 15 Oct. 2010.

Chapter 7. Blame and Violence

1. Johannes Nohl. *The Black Death: A Chronicle of the Plague*. Trans. C. H. Clarke. Yardley, PA: Westholme, 2006. Print. 251.

Chapter 8. The Second Pandemic

1. Philip Ziegler. *The Black Death*. New York: Harper, 1971. Print. 267.

2. Wendy Orent. *Plague: The Mysterious Past and Terrifying Future of the World's Most Dangerous Disease*. New York: Free Press, 2004. Print.163.

3. Patrick Wallis. "A dreadful heritage: Interpreting epidemic disease at Eyam, 1666–2000." *Working Papers on the Nature of Evidence: How Well Do "Facts" Travel?* May 2005. Print. 39.

Chapter 9. A New Era

1. Myron Echenberg. *Plague Ports: The Global Urban Impact of Bubonic Plague, 1894–1901*. New York: New York UP, 2007. Print. 29.

2. Edward Marriott. *Plague: A Story of Science, Rivalry, and the Scourge That Won't Go Away*. New York: Metropolitan, 2003. Print. 151.

INDEX

ABOUT THE AUTHOR

Kevin Cunningham is the author of more than 30 children's books. His books include a series on diseases in history and several books on global disasters. He lives near Chicago.

PHOTO CREDITS

Hulton Archive/Getty Images, cover, 3, 10; North Wind/North Wind Picture Archives, 6, 34, 71, 96, 97 (top); DEA Picture Library/Getty Images, 13; Dennis Kunkel Microscopy, Inc./ Visuals Unlimited/Corbis, 14; CDC/PHIL/Corbis, 18; Ivan Bliznetsov/iStockphoto, 23, 98; Roger Viollet/Getty Images, 24; Stapleton Historical Collection/Photolibrary, 33, 54; Ken Welsh/ Photolibrary, 38; The British Library/Photolibrary, 43, 61; Red Line Editorial, Inc., 44; Max Alexander/Getty Images, 49; Barbara Heller/Photolibrary, 53; After Jan van Eyck/Getty Images, 62; World History Archive/Alamy, 66; Getty Images, 72; Nicole Duplaix/Photolibrary, 79, 82, 99 (bottom); Time Life Pictures/ Mansell/Time Life Pictures/Getty Images, 81, 97 (bottom); Hawaiian Legacy Archive/Photolibrary, 89, 99 (top); National Cancer Institute/Science Faction/Corbis, 95